The fishing disciples

When Jesus grew up, He chose a number of men to help Him teach the people about God. These men were called disciples. Four of them, Peter, Andrew, James and John, were fishermen.

Usually, they went fishing in their boats on the Sea of Galilee, but here they are with their rods, and somehow the lines have become tangled. Can you work out who has caught what?

You can trace the lines with your pen.

If you can decipher this ancient scroll, you will learn the number of Jesus' disciples.

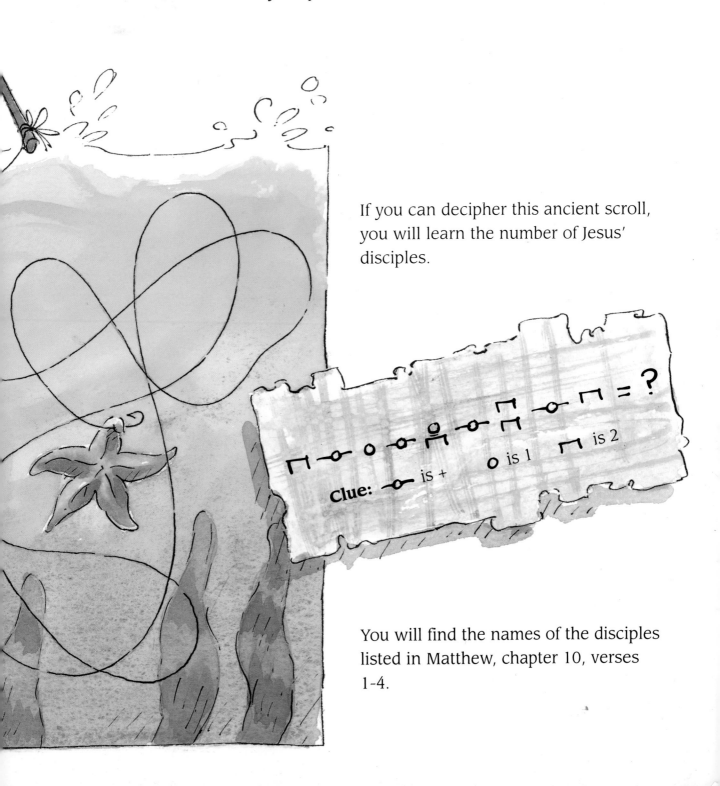

Clue: ⊶ is +   o is 1   ⊓ is 2

You will find the names of the disciples listed in Matthew, chapter 10, verses 1-4.

Feeding the five thousand

One day, when Jesus was out in the countryside, crowds of people gathered round Him to hear Him teach. There were thousands of men, women and children. They stayed, listening to Jesus till late in the evening. At last it was time for them to go home. But the people were hungry; they had not eaten all day.

"Don't send the people away hungry," Jesus told His disciples.

"But where can we get enough food to feed them all?" asked Philip.

"I have five barley loaves and two fishes," said a small boy. Jesus gratefully took the food and blessed it. Then He gave a piece of the bread and fish to each of the hungry people. And they all ate till they were full!

There are 20 deliberate mistakes in this picture. How many of them can you find?

If 2 is B, can you decode these numbers and answer the question? Some of the letters have been put in for you.

8.15.23./13.1.14.25./2.1.19.11.5.20.19./23.5.18.5./6.9.12.12.5.4./
  W   Y   S   E   L   D

23.9.20.8./20.8.5./12.5.6.20./15.22.5.18.19.?
  I H T   F   V   R

If you get stuck, you will find the answer in John, chapter 6, verses 1-13.

The lost sheep

"I am the Good Shepherd," said Jesus.

Sometimes, Jesus told the people a story to help them understand what God is like. This story is about a shepherd who had a hundred sheep.

One day, one of the sheep strayed away and became lost. So the good shepherd left the ninety nine sheep in a safe place and went to search for it.

Can you help him find it? Trace the route with your pen.

When at last the shepherd found the lost sheep, he was so happy, he put it on his shoulders and carried it safely back home.

"In the same way," said Jesus, "there is great happiness in heaven when just one lost person turns to God."

You will find this story in Luke chapter 15, verses 1-7.

The stories Jesus told are called parables. Hidden in the picture are clues of seven other parables. Can you find the clues and name the parables?

HELP!

Finish

Rome

Italy

49

Puteoli

48

48. Slow trek. Throw 1 to reach Rome.

47

Rhegium

46

45

Sicily

Syracuse

44

45. Captain waits for south wind. Miss a turn.

43

Malta

42

41   40   39   38   37   36   35   34

42. Shipwrecked! Swim ashore. Throw 6 to go.

33

32

31

34. Drifting back. Go to 28.

30   29   28   27   26   25   24   23

Phoe

31. S.O.S! Mountain-ous seas. Miss 2 turns.

27. Help! Ship out of control. Go back to 21.

Greece

N

W   E

S